DIRECTED ARROWS

5 FUNDAMENTAL PRINCIPLES
FOR EVERY PARENT

STUDY GUIDE

PRINCIPLE TWO

*The Importance of Knowing Everyone Has
Something They Are Called To Do*

PURPOSE

Deborah V. Morgan

Directed Arrows: 5 Fundamental Principles for Every Parent Study Guide

Copyright © 2020 by Deborah V. Morgan

First Edition

T-XU 2207358

Library of Congress Cataloging-in-Publication Data

ISBN: 978-1-7355418-0-8

Printed in the United States of America

Editing and Design provided by

Marquez Professional Services, LLC

Cover Illustration

Mental Illustration | mental-illustration.com

"For As He Thinks In His Heart, So Is He."
-Proverbs 23:7 (MEV)

Whatever is in your heart dictates what you think. → How you think determines what you do. → What you do affects your destiny.

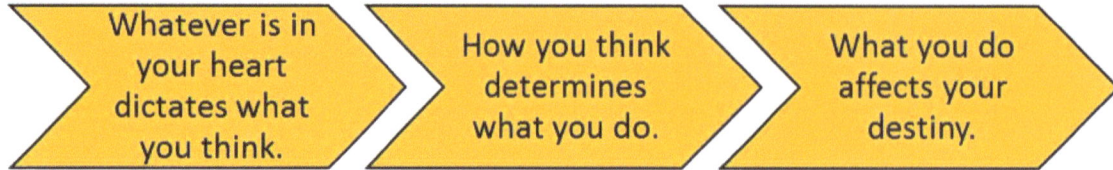

Above all else, guard your heart, for everything you do flows from it.
-Proverbs 4:23 (NIV)

CONTENTS

INTRODUCTION

We all love receiving gifts. Gifts make people smile. We get them for our birthdays, holidays, and sometimes for no special reason at all. A gift is "something given voluntarily without payment in return." Can you think of the best gift you have ever received? What about the best gift you have ever given?

John 3:16 tells us, "For God so loved the world He gave His one and only Son, that whoever believes in Him shall not perish but have eternal life." The motivation behind God's giving is always love. The reason I asked about the best gift you have ever given is that I believe the greatest gift you can give to your family is YOU!

Many times, we do not see ourselves as gifts. We struggle with our past, our insecurities, our fears, lack of self-love, and even our unforgiving hearts. Whatever we store up in our hearts will manifest in our thoughts and actions. As God is our example, we, too, should be motivated by love. We should love God, love ourselves so that we can properly love our family. The family structure is so important that Psalm 68:6 (NIV), tells us, "God sets the lonely in families."

The Bible is full of valuable principles God shared with us because He knows us. He created us. His love caused Him to provide a manual of instructions for daily living. He "KNOWS ALL THINGS." So, nothing catches Him off guard or makes Him nervous.

Micah 6:8 (NCV), explains what He requires from us. "The Lord has told you, human, what is good; he has told you what he wants from you: to do what is right to other people, love being kind to others, and live humbly, obeying your God." Sounds easy, right? As humans, we tend to complicate matters that God has addressed. Take, for instance, parenting.

Directed Arrows, 5 Fundamental Principles for Every Parent, is a book that explores the subject of parenting from biblical wisdom found in Psalm 127. In this family Psalm, God has given us a pattern to follow for blessings in our homes. The family is only as strong as its foundation. So, we must build our families on biblical principles. The book, Directed Arrows explains five fundamental principles, and in this study guide, we will explore Principle Two, Purpose.

Are you ready to be empowered to be the individual and the family God called you to be? If you answered yes! Let's begin.

FROM THE HEART

Throughout the study guide, you will find a vignette focusing on one moment in my life as a mother, youth leader, and director of a childcare center. When you see this arrow heart shape symbol, it indicates my personal stories, experiences, and lessons learned.

I must emphasize that the most important decision I ever made was to have a personal relationship with Jesus Christ. I can tell you that having this relationship with Him is extremely valuable and necessary as you maneuver throughout the various aspects of parenting.

I pray the time you spend completing the study guide will be helpful, bring insight, and empower you to enjoy your parenting journey.

THE 5 PRINCIPLES

PRINCIPLE 1   **PRIORITIES**

The importance of giving God first place in your life.

PRINCIPLE 2   **PURPOSE**

The importance of knowing everyone has something they are called to do.

PRINCIPLE 3   **PRODUCTIVE**

The importance of time management.

PRINCIPLE 4   **POWER**

The importance of being resilient.

PRINCIPLE 5   **PROFIT**

The importance of your legacy.

PSALM 127 (GW)

1. If the LORD does not build the house, it is useless for the builders to work on it. If the LORD does not protect a city, it is useless for the guard to stay alert.

2. It is useless to work hard for the food you eat by getting up early and going to bed late. The LORD gives food to those He loves while they sleep.

3. Children are an inheritance from the LORD. They are a reward from Him.

4. The children born to a man when he is young are like arrows in the hand of a warrior.

5. Blessed is the man who has filled his quiver with them. He will not be put to shame when he speaks with his enemies in the gate.

Purpose

This is a study guide that focuses on Principle Two, Purpose. The design is recommended to be completed after you have read the book, *Directed Arrows, 5 Fundamental Principles for Every Parent*. This is book two in a series of five study guides that correlate with each of the five principles. Prayerfully the study guide will help you develop and apply the principles into your daily living.

Isaiah 49:2 (NIV) says, "He made my mouth like a sharpened sword, in the shadow of his hand he hid me; he made me into a polished arrow and concealed me in his quiver." This verse uses the word 'made' twice. God is the Creator of everything, and He knows the purpose He has for His creations. If you want to know your purpose, you should consult with your Maker.

Psalm 127 is the anchor scripture for this study guide. This Psalm has five verses which translates into five essential principles for every person on the planet. When these principles are applied, you will see growth and transformation in your life and in your family. According to the Bible, transformation occurs when you renew your mind (Romans 12:2). Renewing your mind affects the way you think and conduct your life. This is done by help from the Holy Spirit. Having a personal relationship with Jesus Christ is extremely valuable and necessary as you maneuver through life and the various aspects of parenting. Proverbs 23:7 reminds us, *"For as he thinks in his heart, so is he."* How you think dictates the direction of your life. My desire for you as you explore and meditate on these verses is that the trajectory of your life is forever changed. As you take this journey of discovery, seek God for guidance, spend time in prayer, and let Him reveal what you are called to do. What your child/children are called to do. May you live and parent with **PURPOSE!**

YOUR HAVE PURPOSE

We know everything, and every person created has a purpose, from the tiniest insect to people, to the most complicated machinery. It is the Maker of a product that determines its purpose and function. So, what is your purpose? What were you created to do?

Before you were born, God had a plan for you in His mind. Each one of us was born with a calling to fulfill. Every day you should seek Him to discover how you fit into His amazing plan for the world. It is frustrating when you spend countless hours doing things you were never created to do. The Bible conveys truth in James 1:5, "If you lack wisdom, you should ask God." God provides answers to many of our complex questions (Like what's my purpose?) However, we must be sensitive enough to hear what He's saying. God speaks through a variety of ways, mainly through His Word, the Bible. But don't limit Him. He will use your dreams, a billboard, a radio show, information from a book, or through another person.

Believe it or not, you have a unique gift from God and the world needs it. He created you to make a positive impact and bring good to this world. You may have a gift for communication, science, arts, education, administration, or encouragement for others. Whatever your purpose, it connects with God's purpose. As you read and study His Word, you will learn what His true purpose is all about.

Wherever you have influence, **GO** make a difference! Someone is waiting for you. Your family is waiting for you! Are you living every day on PURPOSE?

> *Isaiah 49:1 (NIV): "Listen to me, you islands; hear this, you distant nations: Before I was born the Lord called me; from my mother's womb he has spoken my name."*

How remarkable! To know the Lord had special plans for your child even before you brought them into this world.

Do you believe every person is born into this world to make a difference? Why or Why not?

_____

_____

_____

Romans 12:6 (NLT) says, "In his grace, God has given us different gifts for doing certain things well." What are some things you believe you do well? What were you born to do?

_____

_____

_____

Many people want to know the purpose and meaning of life. Most importantly, they want to discover *their* purpose in life. I believe as our roles change, so does our purpose and assignments from God. They may be connected and prepare you for the next phase in your life. When you decide to start your family, your purpose shifts to include purpose and destiny for each person in your family. Family planning is worthwhile work! Planning and raising a family require effort, courage, and prayer.

> **Quote:** *"Efforts and courage are not enough without purpose and direction"*
>
> ~ John F. Kennedy

What does this statement mean to you?

_____

_____

_____

_____

Most individuals do not have a well thought out plan before starting a family or for raising children.

Do you or did you have a family plan? (Circle) YES or NO

> » Examples for discussion:
>
> » How will you discipline your children?
>
> » Will they attend private or public schools?
>
> » Will you establish a college fund?
>
> » What family traditions will you create?

What's
the
plan?

Define these words:

Effort:

_____

_____

_____

Courage:

_____

_____

_____

Prayer:

_____

_____

_____

It's never too late to create a family plan. You can always start fresh where you are. You need clear and precise instructions for the journey of parenting. Bear in mind, hard work, effort, and courage will unquestionably help you reach your envisioned goals. It's always best to start with prayer. We must train ourselves to invite the LORD into every area of our life first. "Many are the plans in a person's heart, but it is the Lord's purpose that prevails" (Proverbs 19:21, NIV).

What is the value of having a plan? Should plans be flexible?

_____

_____

_____

_____

What are some things you will consider in developing a family plan?

_____

_____

_____

_____

What are some things you will incorporate immediately in your family?

_____

_____

_____

_____

How does Principle One-Priorities affect your planning?

_____

_____

"IN VAINYOU RISE UP EARLY AND STAY UP LATE, EATING THE BREAD OF TOIL, FOR HE PROVIDES FOR HIS BELOVED ONES EVEN IN THEIR SLEEP."- PSALM 127:2 (TLV)

Psalm 127:2 is not saying work is in vain: King Solomon is revealing a secret; you can work with anxiety or tranquility. Applying Principle One, Priorities will help with having peace of mind.

Are you stretched and stressed with the daily cares of life and have little energy left for your family? Your children? How can you apply the secret of Psalm 127:2 to your life?

_____

_____

_____

_____

_____

> *"Think about the peace we forfeit when we lack trust in God to lead us through all types of circumstance that find their way into our lives."*

How does having trust in God relate to purpose, peace, plans, and parenting?

Do you have peace in your home? If not, what can you do to bring peace?

_____

_____

_____

_____

What are some benefits of creating a peaceful home?

_____

_____

_____

_____

QUIET ZONE

As a parent, you need time to rest. It is important to create a personal place and time where you can relax. God wants your wholehearted attention so He can share His heart with you. During your quiet time, God can give you insight, answer questions, and reveal His purpose. We must make space for Him in our action-packed lives.

Do you think action-packed lives interfere with the quality of family time? How so?

_____

_____

_____

_____

Describe your typical day.

_____

_____

_____

_____

Do you have personal quiet time? If not, will you incorporate quiet time now?

_____

_____

_____

_____

Have you set aside a special time and place to meet with God? How can you and your family

benefit from this practice?

_____

_____

_____

_____

What would you like to share with God in prayer today?

_____

_____

_____

_____

Prayer

Read Psalm 16:7 (NCV). What insight did you receive from this passage?

_____

_____

_____

_____

Make a list of questions you have for God?

1.

2.

3.

4.

5.

Journal how you feel right now.

_____

_____

_____

_____

_____

_____

God Has a Purpose for Every Person

PURPOSE: "THE REASON FOR WHICH SOMETHING EXISTS OR IS
DONE, MADE, USED, ETC. "

The origin of the word is a derivative of the Old French porpos, which means intention, aim, or goal.

===

The prophets Isaiah and Jeremiah express the same thought before they were born, God chose, formed, knew, set apart, and appointed them. Again, I repeat, God has a plan and a purpose for every person. No one is a mistake. No matter how they got here.

Have you ever asked the questions, "what is my purpose?" "What should I be doing with my life?" What came to mind?

_____

_____

_____

_____

How does knowing and embracing the truth of God's Word help with discovering your purpose? Your family's purpose? Your child's purpose?

_____

_____

_____

_____

_____

Unfortunately, children do not come with instructions when you bring them home from the hospital. And even if we had a detailed list to follow, we would still experience challenges attempting to raise them, as no child is precisely like another. However, The Bible is an essential "manual" full of instructions for raising children as you guide your child to hit the mark of God's amazing plan for their life.

How can you discover God's purpose for you? Your family? Your children?

_____

_____

_____

What are some things you know God has called you to do as it relates to being a parent?

_____

_____

_____

The Bible is full of wisdom, direction, and instruction to support you as you guide your child. Ultimately, you will have to take time to discover the make-up of your child and study God's "manual" to point them toward the path He has chosen from them to follow and make a difference in the world. What instructions are you familiar with from the Bible regarding family/ children?

_____

_____

_____

_____

The Journey of Discovery

"The journey of discovery will involve time, patience, and diligence; it is a seeking process. To seek, means "to go in search of or discover by searching or questioning." You must do some serious digging to learn how to find the treasures hidden deep within your child."

List some treasures you have discovered about your child (children).

Child's Name	Treasure Discovered

Take time to study God's manual (The Bible). When you search the Scriptures, ask questions. Questions will lead to a better understanding of purpose and bring clarity.

» What type of parents do you see in the Bible?

» What is God's design for the family?

» Do you relate to any family in the Bible?

» What are some family situations you find interesting?

» What lessons and messages can you learn?

» Do you need to make changes in your family? Your parenting style?

» How does God reveal Himself and His purpose for individuals?

Nuggets of Wisdom

Keep your eyes and ears open for God's nuggets of wisdom!

James 1:5 says, "If you lack wisdom, you should ask God." Wisdom, knowledge, and understanding are three significant vehicles for parenting. They will carry you where you need to go on the road of parenthood. The book of Proverbs is best known for providing Godly wisdom and strategies for righteous living.

Read Proverbs 4:6-9. What parental strategy can you identify?

_____

_____

_____

_____

_____

_____

_____

NOTE TO PARENTS:

"You do not have to struggle to determine the purpose of your child. Your focus should be to aid in their discovery of it. You are responsible for leading, directing and helping your child reach their full potential and carry out the mission they were designed to fulfill."

There have been many times in my life I had questions for God. I asked questions about myself, my family members, my job, and even explanations of some scriptures I did not fully understand. God would answer my questions in the oddest ways!

I used to commute 30-40 minutes to work and church. In my travel times, I would listen to talk radio and Christian talk radio stations. And more than once, the topic would be on a question I asked God. I would get my answer, and then cry and praise God all the way to work. Many times, I had to sit in the parking lot and reapply my make-up before going in. I don't have a poker face so some of the more observant staff members would ask, "are you ok? Have you been crying?" And I would reply, "God is Good!"

Believe it or not, one day, He answered me through a billboard sign as I was driving on the highway! You have to be open to the ways God uses. Don't box Him in. He can use anything to get a message or an answer to you.

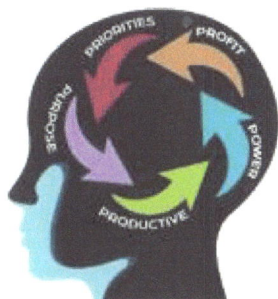

"For as he thinks in his heart, so is he." Proverbs 23:7 (MEV)

Everyone has a unique gift; and are born into this world to make a difference. God made your child and knows the envisioned plan for which they were created. Parents should not force children to do things they were never created to do. You may have your own plans and desires for them; however, God has a set course for your child to follow. Your focus should be on discovering what God's plan is for them. Do not limit them because of your desires, watch them, and see what comes naturally to them. Be their biggest supporter and let them explore and find out their interest and passion. Teach them the importance of serving. Serving God and serving others.

Proverbs 22:6 (MSG) says, *"Point your kids in the right direction-when they're old, they won't be lost."* As your children are growing up, YOU should have the strongest influence in their life. Children are not equipped to make informed decisions that may regulate the course of life they will go on without your counsel. Spending time with God in prayer is necessary to help you guide them. It's helpful to explain how their purpose is connected to God's purposes and plan for our world.

It is of vital importance that you do not allow anything or anyone to compromise your child's purpose. Convey to them how to live by divine standards and develop relationships with others who are similar minded. Likewise, help them understand their value and worth to you and God.

Each family member receives a **unique** gift and assignment from God. Remember, you are not determining their path; you are noticing their natural bents. You were born with a "calling." And that "calling" includes serving others.

DEFINITION: **CALLING**- "A STRONG URGE TOWARD A PARTICULAR
WAY OF LIFE OR CAREER; A VOCATION."

Read Psalm 139:14. What does it mean to be "fearfully and wonderfully made?"

_____

_____

_____

_____

Parents should tell their children how important they are not only to you, but to God as well. I believe this gives them a sense of worth and will help guide their choices as they mature. Use the Bible to share stories with them. Explain how they can learn valuable lessons from the lives of others.

What unique gifts and talents have you noticed in your child/children? What comes naturally to them?

_____

_____

_____

_____

Examples:

- » Leadership, Organization, Administration

- » Sports, Music, Dance

- » Art, Reading, Writing

- » Math, Science, Hospitality

How are you cultivating your child's gifts?

_____

_____

_____

_____

Do you encourage your child/children to do things they are naturally equipped to do?

Try new things?

_____

_____

_____

_____

What plans or goals have you set for your child and/or family?

_____

_____

_____

_____

Do your children see you enjoying your purpose? Do you talk about purpose with them?

_____

_____

_____

_____

"If children do not have parental guidance, they will look to the opinions of their friends, social media, and secular ideologies for direction."

Do you believe associations with others can influence one's purpose? Why or Why not?

_____

_____

_____

_____

Do you know who your child considers as a "role model?" What qualities does this person have that your child admires? Ask them why?

_____

_____

_____

_____

_____

Why is it important to pray for wisdom as it relates to your child's purpose?

_____

_____

_____

_____

List individuals who give you wise parental advice.

1 _____   2 _____   3 _____

"It is eaiser to build strong children than to repair broken men." -Frederick Douglass

What does this statement mean to you?

_____

_____

_____

_____

In my class titled, "Youth and Crime" from Indiana Wesleyan University, one assignment stated the following: "If a young person can articulate goals, he or she is less likely to be involved in criminal activity. What can be done to give a purpose to youths who appear to have no hope?" These questions were thought-provoking. Again, people want to know their purpose. It reminded me of why I feel so strongly about the need of parents to communicate with their children God's plan for their lives.

Why do you think young people who have goals and know their purpose are less involved in delinquent behaviors?

_____

_____

_____

_____

_____

How can you help another family who may be facing challenges with their child/children with what you have learned so far?

_____

_____

_____

_____

_____

You should never compare yourself, your child/children, or your family with another. Every person and every family has its unique purpose of fulfilling. Each family member has a specific contribution necessary to help it operate sufficiently. Although there is no perfect family, because there are no perfect people (we all have flaws), perfection is in the "striving" to fulfill the plans God has for your family.

What's the danger of comparing your family to another?

_____

_____

_____

_____

What's the danger of comparing your children to others?

_____

_____

_____

_____

How can you help another family who may be facing challenges with their child/children with what you have learned so far?

_____

_____

_____

How do you handle your child's negative behavior? Negative attitudes?

_____

_____

_____

How can the world benefit   when individuals and families are living with and on purpose?

_____

_____

_____

_____

"Not all of us can do great things. But we can do small things with great love."

-Mother Teresa

Prayer Is A Necessity For Your Family

Write a prayer asking God to reveal His purpose for your family. Make sure you include the date of your prayer. It's always good to go back and reflect on your prayers.

POINTS TO RECALL

» Planning and raising a family require effort, courage, purpose, and direction.

» When you develop a strategic plan, and your purpose is well defined, you are more apt to reach the intended goal with less unexpected obstacles.

» God has a purpose for which He created you and your child.

» You do not have to determine your child's purpose; you are there to aid in their discovery of it.

Define "purpose" in your own words.

_____

_____

_____

_____

Do you understand how valuable you are for guiding your child toward God's intended purpose for their life?

_____

_____

_____

_____

_____

_____

Do you see the significance and value of your role and responsibility in your child's life? In your family?

_____

_____

_____

_____

_____

Will you reexamine your family's plan? What will you add or remove?

_____

_____

_____

_____

How does _your_ purpose connect with God's amazing plan? Your _family's_ purpose?

_____

_____

_____

_____

_____

Things To Think About

What will you incorporate into your life and your family from the study of Principle Two?

_____

_____

_____

_____

What are you going to do differently after completing this study guide?

_____

_____

_____

_____

How can you and your family impact the lives of other families?

_____

_____

_____

_____

Do you feel empowered to challenge your family to live on purpose? Take what you are doing to another level?

_____

_____

_____

_____

Read and reflect on the following verses. What practical application will you apply to your life and family?

Psalm 127:2

_____

_____

_____

_____

Isaiah 49:1

_____

_____

_____

_____

Jeremiah 1:5

_____

_____

_____

Romans 12:6

_____

_____

_____

Proverbs 23:7

_____

_____

_____

Proverbs 22:6

_____

_____

_____

Proverbs 20:5

_____

_____

_____

1 Peter 2:9

_____

_____

_____

Colossians 3:17

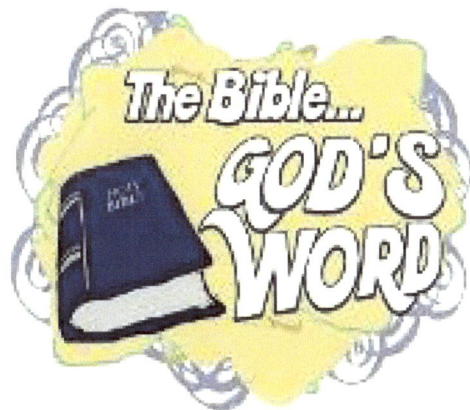

_____

_____

_____

Prayer Is A Necessity For Your Family

Write a prayer regarding understanding how to guide your child/children toward God's purpose for their life.

Personal Notes:

_____

_____

_____

_____

_____

_____

_____

_____

_____

_____

_____

_____

_____

_____

_____

Personal Notes:

Personal Notes:

_____

_____

_____

_____

_____

_____

_____

_____

_____

_____

_____

_____

_____

THE 5 FUNDAMENTAL PRINCIPLES FOR EVERY PARENT

PRIORITIES

Establishing God's primary importance in the family.

PURPOSE

Discovering God's plan for each family member

PRODUCTIVE

Accomplishing good works.

POWER

Building resilience in the family.

PROFIT

Leaving a lifelong legacy reaping the rewards.

"Yesterday is gone. Tomorrow has not yet come. We have only today. Let us begin."

-Mother Teresa

Thank You!

It has been a pleasure to prepare this study guide for you. I hope you and your family are forever changed as you make God the priority of your life and your home. I pray you are inspired to share what God has made real to you with your friends and other family members. We can impact our world one family at a time. May God's blessings be upon you as you Parent with Purpose!

Deborah V. Morgan

The family is only as strong as its foundation.

God has given us a pattern to follow for blessings in our homes. Psalm 127 is where you will discover five fundamental principles for parenting. Directed Arrows encourages parents to see how valuable they are and the importance of directing their children toward God's intended purpose.

"FOR AS HE THINKS IN HIS HEART, SO IS HE."

PROVERBS 23:7 (MEV)

ABOUT THE AUTHOR

Deborah V. Morgan was born in Warren, Ohio. With her husband Darren, she raised three daughters, Dominique, Diona, and Darice, in the surrounding areas of Cleveland, Ohio. She currently resides in Atlanta, Georgia, where she answered the call to create study guides to enhance the truths in her book, Directed Arrows: 5 Fundamental Principles for Every Parent.